WHEN YOU FEEL LIKE GIVING UP

REMEMBER WHY YOU HELD ON

FOR SO LONG IN THE FIRST PLACE

THERE IS NO FAILURE EXCEPT
IN NO LONGER TRYING

Place your Quote here

Write your Future Goals

NEVER STOP TRYING. NEVER STOP BELIEVING

NEVER GIVE UP
YOUR DAY WILL COME

DRAW HERE

THINGS AREN'T ALWAYS EASY,
BUT YOU JUST HAVE TO KEEP GOING
AND
DON'T LET THE SMALL STUFF BOG YOU DOWN

Place your Quote here

Write your Future Goals

____

____

____

____

____

I REFUSE TO QUIT BECAUSE I HAVEN'T TRIED ALL POSSIBLE WAYS YET

NEVER GIVE UP
ON SOMETHING YOU BELIEVE IN

Place your Quote here

Write your Future Goals

IT IS NOT WANTING TO WIN THAT MAKES YOU A WINNER IT IS REFUSING TO FAIL

DRAW HERE

DON'T GIVE UP BEFORE
THE MIRACLE HAPPENS

Place your Quote here

Write your Future Goals

YOU'RE A FIGHTER
LOOK AT EVERYTHING
YOU'VE OVERCOME
DON'T GIVE UP NOW

DRAW HERE

THERE IS NO SUBSTITUTE
FOR HARD WORK
HARD WORK

Place your Quote here

Write your Future Goals

IT'S HARD TO BEAT A PERSON

WHO NEVER GIVES UP

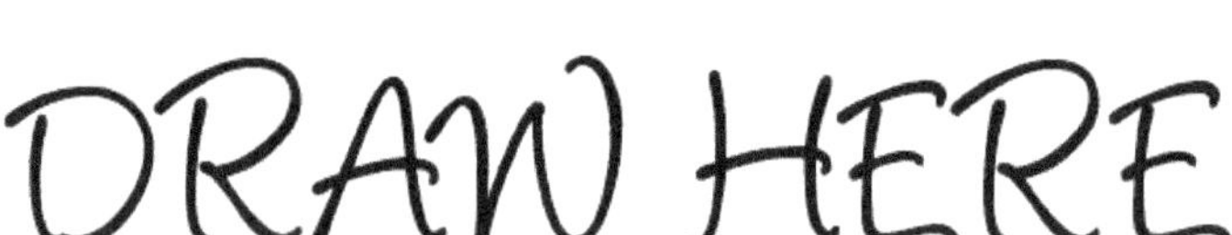

DRAW HERE

YOU NEVER GIVE UP
EVEN WHEN YOU SHOULD

Place your Quote here

Write your Future Goals

I NEVER LOSE

I EITHER WIN OR LEARN

DRAW HERE

DON'T LISTEN TO WHAT ANYBODY SAYS
EXCEPT THE PEOPLE WHO ENCOURAGE YOU
IF IT'S WHAT YOU WANT TO DO
AND IT'S WITHIN YOURSELF
THEN KEEP GOING AND TRY TO DO IT
FOR THE REST OF YOUR LIFE

Place your Quote here

Write your Future Goals

FALL SEVEN TIMES STAND UP EIGHT

DRAW HERE

OUR GREATEST WEAKNESS LIES IN GIVING UP
THE MOST CERTAIN WAY TO SUCCEED
IS ALWAYS TO TRY JUST ONE MORE TIME

Place your Quote here

Write your Future Goals

____

____

____

____

PERSEVERANCE IS FAILING 19 TIMES

AND

SUCCEEDING THE 20TH

DRAW HERE

SOMETIMES ADVERSITY IS WHAT YOU HAVE

TO FACE IN ORDER TO BECOME SUCCESSFUL

DRAW HERE